ISBN 0-7935-3884-X

PUBLISHING

EXCLUSIVELY DISTRIBUTED BY

7777 W. BLUEMOUND RD. P.O. BOX 13819 MILWAUKEE, WI 53213

IMAGINE™
John Lennon®

REAL LOVE

Words and Music
by JOHN LENNON

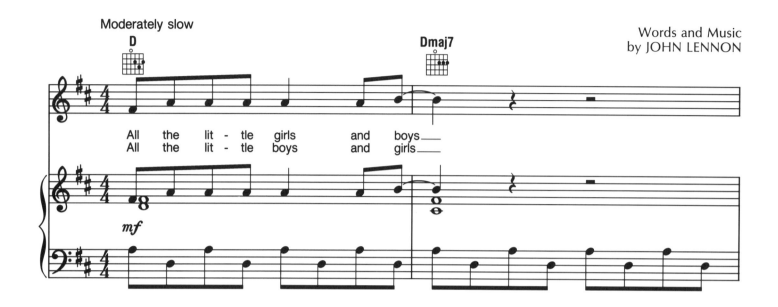

Moderately slow

All the lit - tle girls and boys___
All the lit - tle boys and girls___

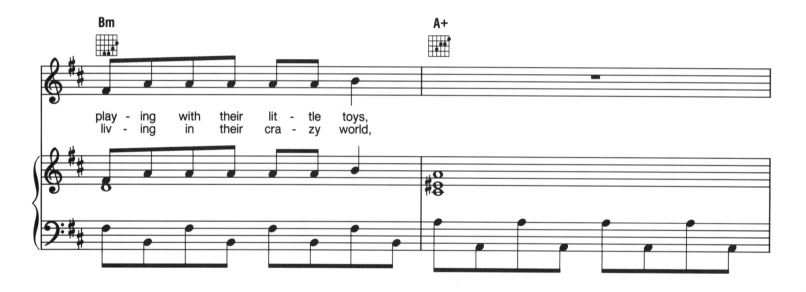

play - ing with their lit - tle toys,
liv - ing in their cra - zy world,

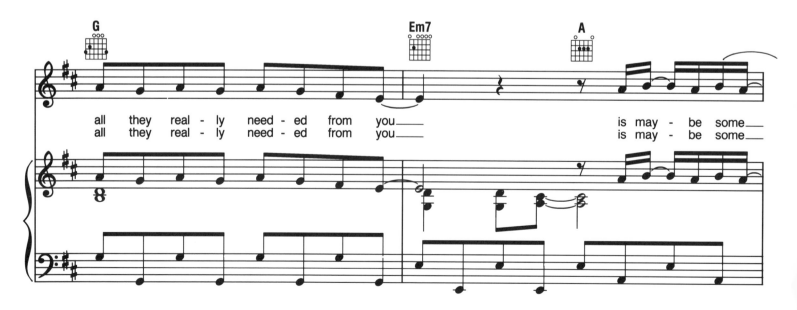

all they real - ly need - ed from you___   is may - be some___
all they real - ly need - ed from you___   is may - be some___

whistle

don't ex - pect for you_____ to____ un - der - stand,____

7

IN MY LIFE

Words and Music by
JOHN LENNON and PAUL McCARTNEY

TWIST AND SHOUT

Moderately with a beat

Words and Music by BERT RUSSELL
and PHIL MEDLEY

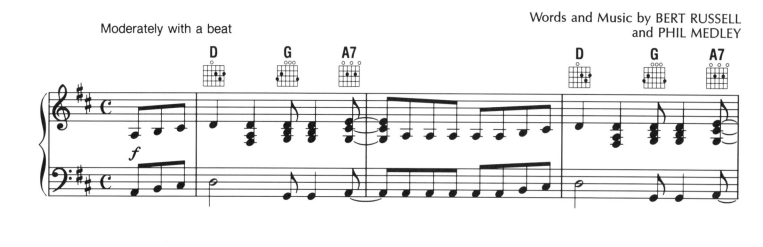

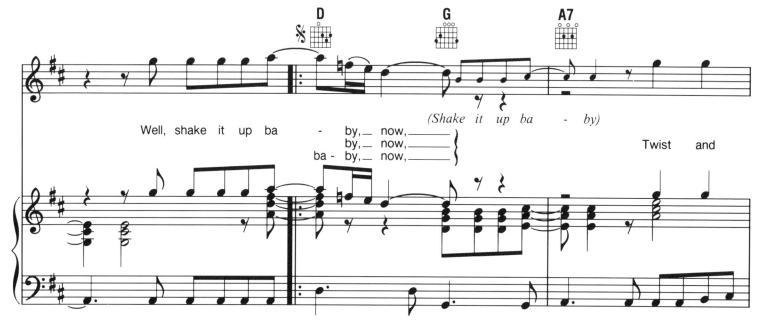

Well, shake it up ba - by,__ now,_____
ba - by,__ now,_____
(Shake it up ba - by)

Twist and

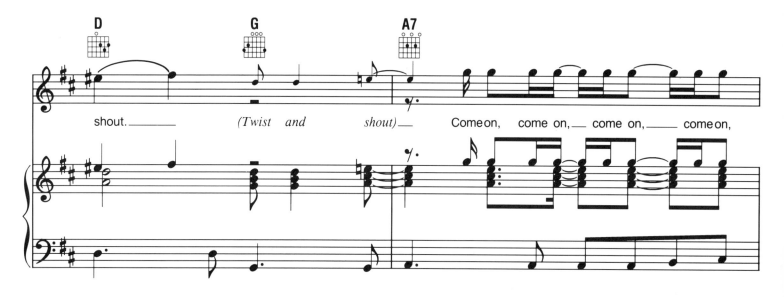

shout._____
*(Twist and shout)*__
Come on, come on,__ come on,___ come on,

HELP!

Moderately, with a driving beat

Words and Music by
JOHN LENNON and PAUL McCARTNEY

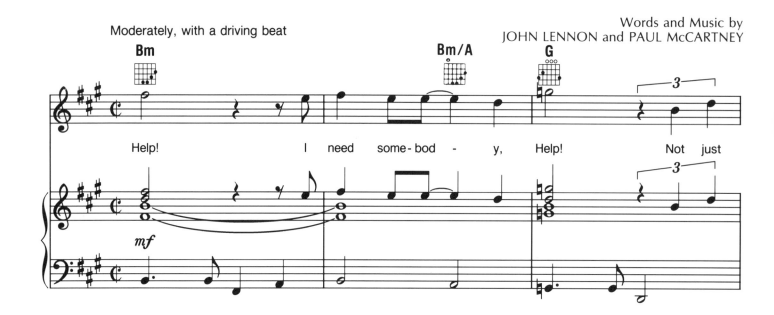

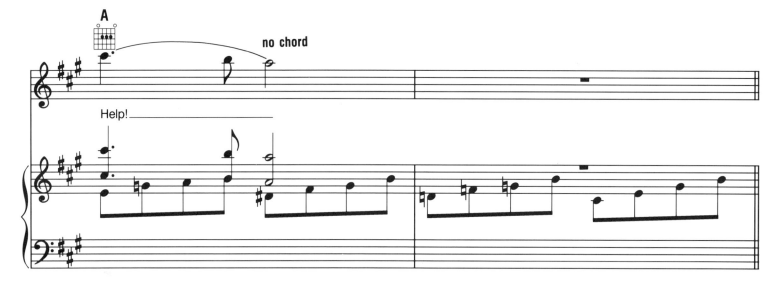

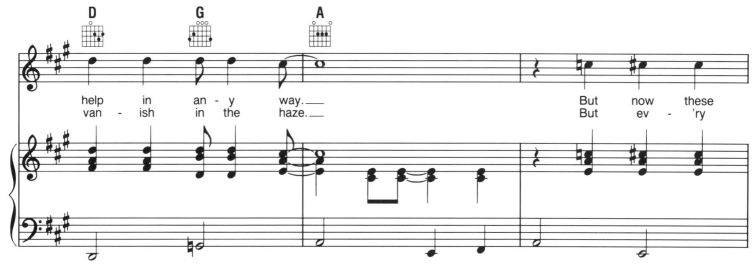

Now I find   I've changed my mind,   I've o - pened up the doors.

I know that I   just need you like   I've nev - er   done be - fore.

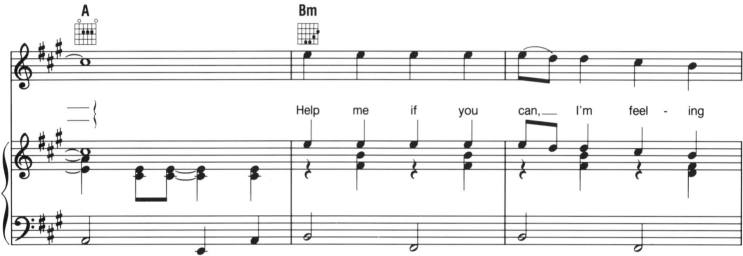

Help me if you can,   I'm feel - ing

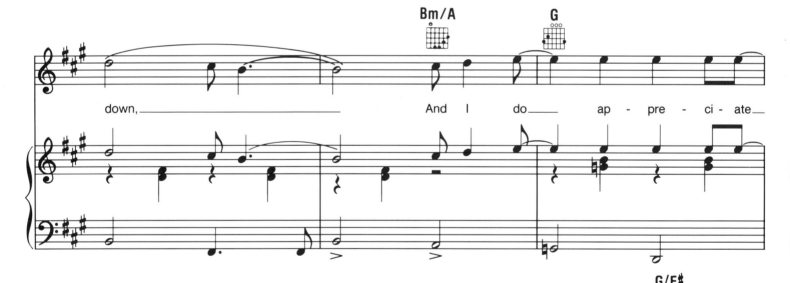

down,   And I do   ap - pre - ci - ate

you be - ing 'round.

STRAWBERRY FIELDS FOREVER

Words and Music by
JOHN LENNON and PAUL McCARTNEY

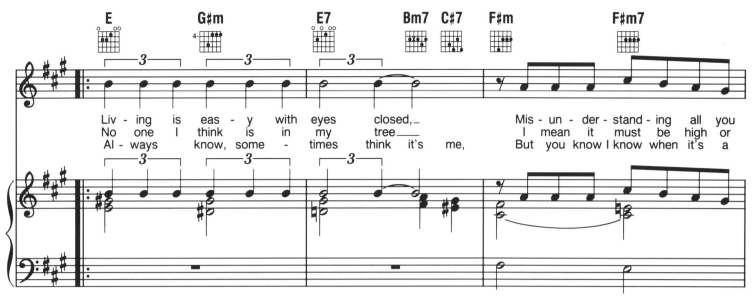

Liv - ing is eas - y with eyes closed,—
No one I think is in my tree—
Al - ways know, some - times think it's me,
Mis - un - der - stand - ing all you
I mean it must be high or
But you know I know when it's a

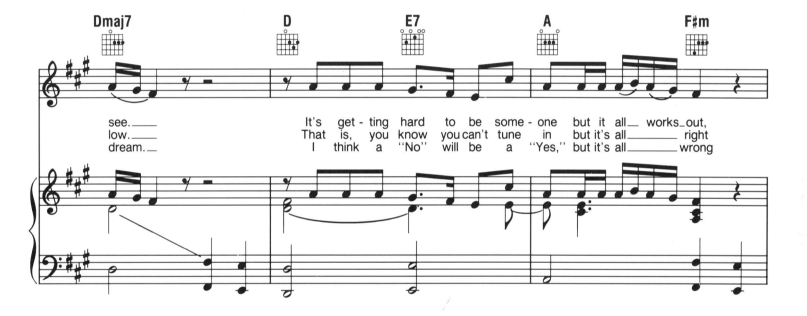

see.—
low.—
dream.—
It's get - ting hard to be some - one but it all— works— out,
That is, you know you can't tune in but it's all— right
I think a "No" will be a "Yes," but it's all— wrong

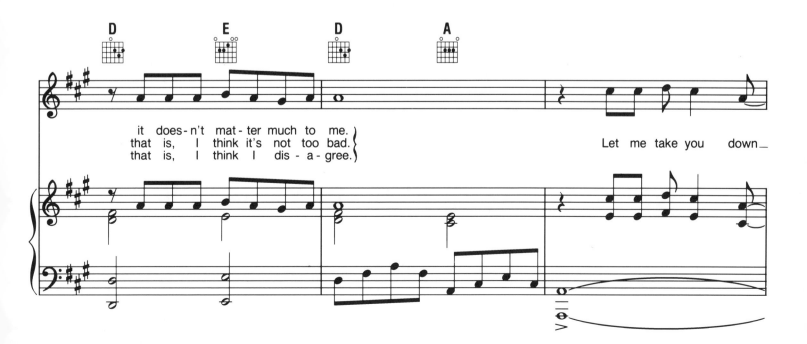

it does - n't mat - ter much to me. }
that is, I think it's not too bad. }
that is, I think I dis - a - gree. }

Let me take you down—

THE BALLAD OF JOHN AND YOKO

Words and Music by
JOHN LENNON and PAUL McCARTNEY

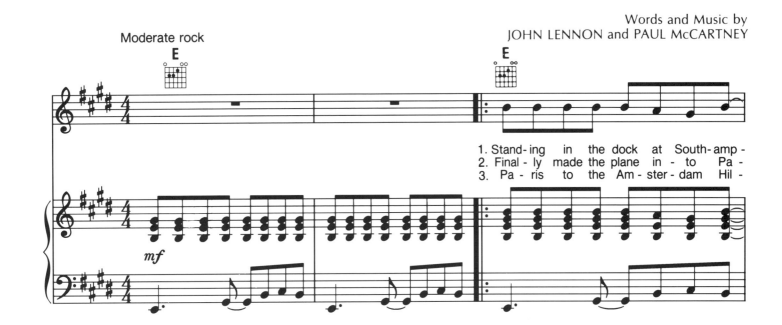

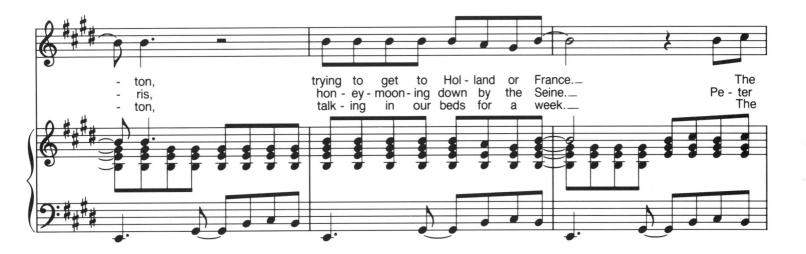

24

Sav - ing up your mon - ey for a rain - y day,

giv-ing all your clothes to char - i - ty.

Last night the wife said,

"Oh boy, when you're dead you don't take noth-ing with you but your soul." _____ Think!

4. Made a light - ning trip to Vi - en - na,
5. Caught the ear - ly plane back to Lon - don,

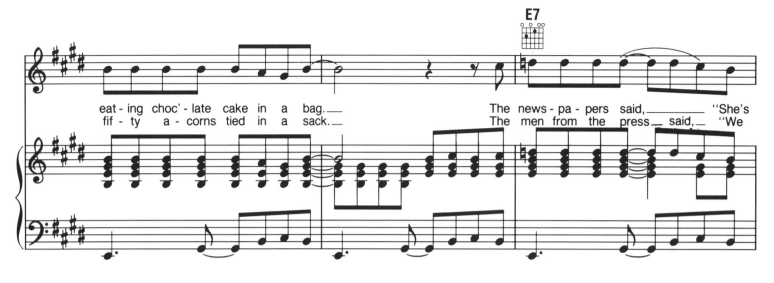

eat - ing choc' - late cake in a bag.___ The news - pa - pers said,___ "She's
fif - ty a - corns tied in a sack.___ The men from the press___ said,___ "We

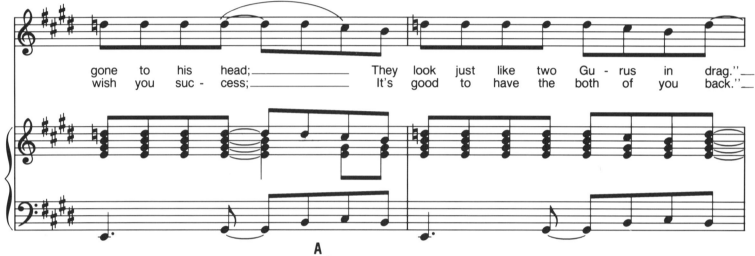

gone to his head;_____ They look just like two Gu - rus in drag."
wish you suc - cess;_____ It's good to have the both of you back."

___{Christ! You know it ain't eas - y,___ you know how hard it can be.___

___ The way things are go - ing___

A DAY IN THE LIFE

Words and Music by
JOHN LENNON and PAUL McCARTNEY

way down - stairs and drank a cup, and look-ing up I no-ticed I was late.

Found my coat and grabbed my hat__ made the bus in sec-onds

flat. Found my way up - stairs and had a smoke and

some-bod-y spoke and I went in-to a dream. Ah__

REVOLUTION

Words and Music by
JOHN LENNON and PAUL McCARTNEY

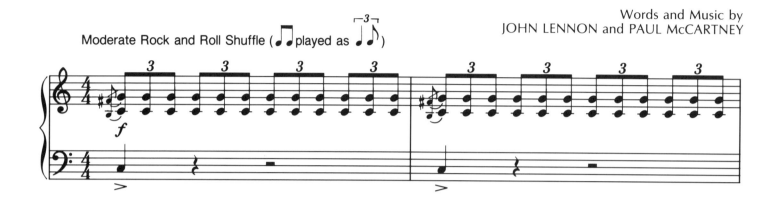

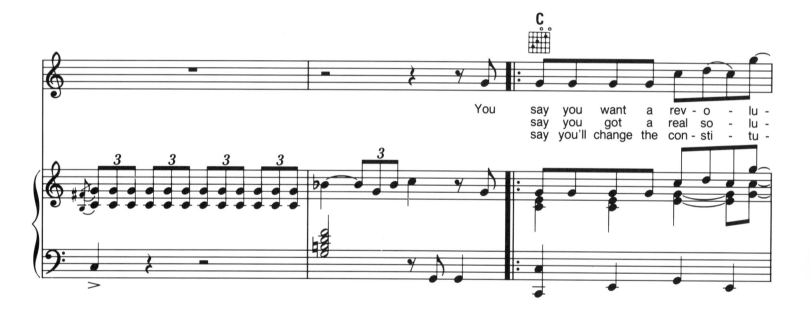

JULIA

Words and Music by
JOHN LENNON and PAUL McCARTNEY

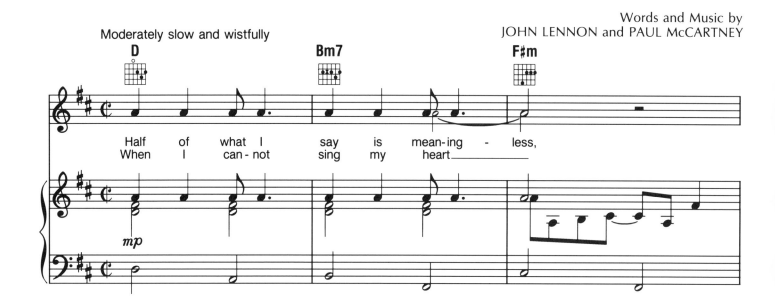

Moderately slow and wistfully

Half of what I say is mean-ing - less,
When I can - not sing my heart ____

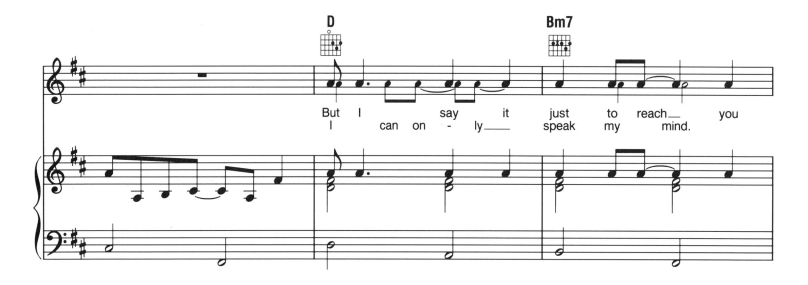

But I say it just to reach ____ you
I can on - ly ____ just speak my reach mind.

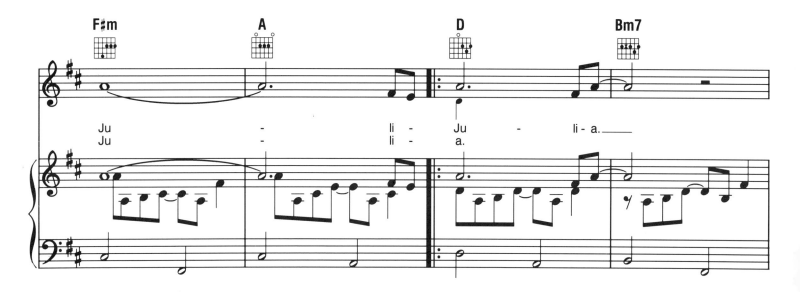

Ju - li - a Ju - li - a. ____
Ju - li - a.

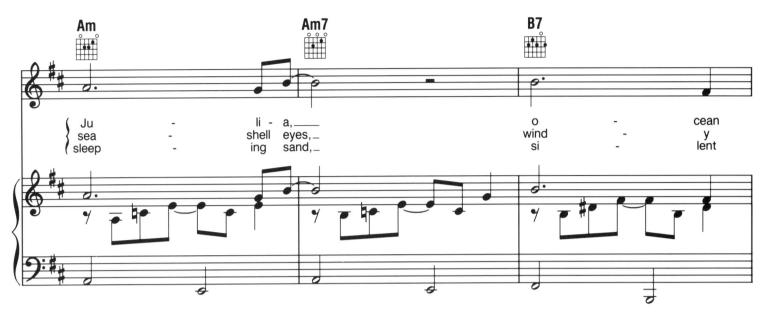

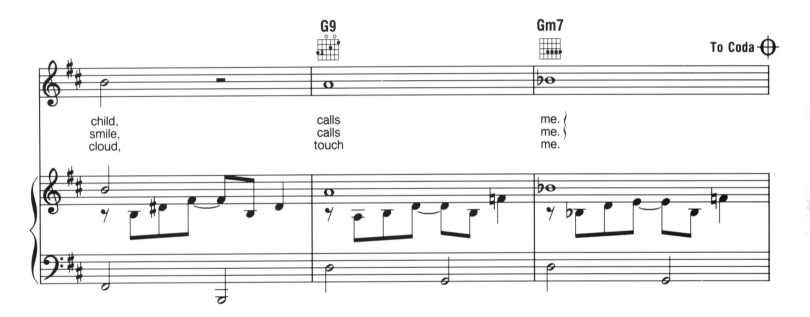

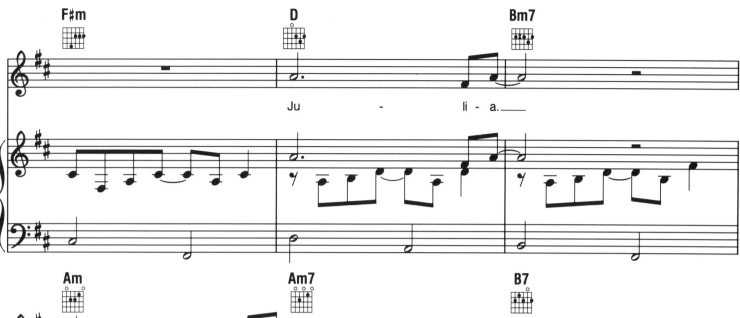

Ju - li - a.

Ju - li - a,___ morn - ing

moon touch me.

So I sing a song___ of love,___ Ju -

D.C. al Coda

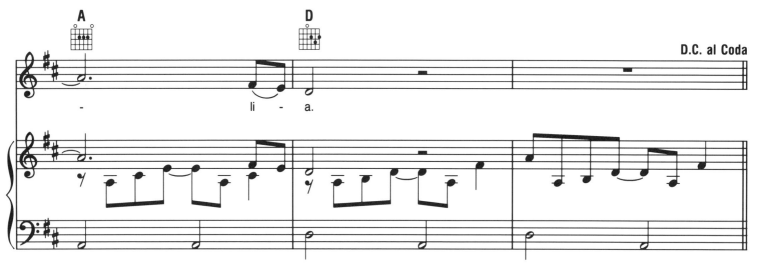

li - a.

CODA

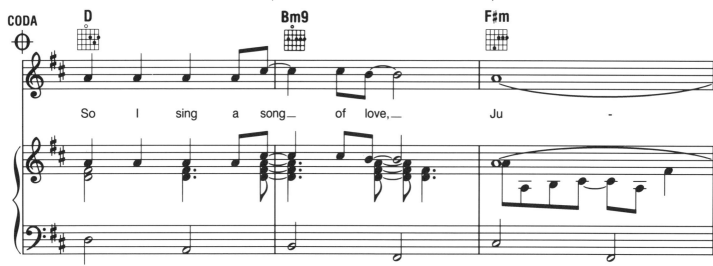

So I sing a song of love, Ju -

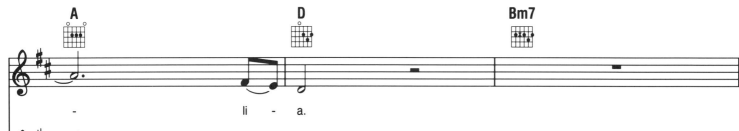

li - a.

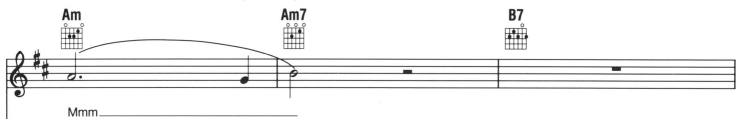

Mmm _____

DON'T LET ME DOWN

Words and Music by
JOHN LENNON and PAUL McCARTNEY

GIVE PEACE A CHANCE

Words and Music by JOHN LENNON
and PAUL McCARTNEY

Is - n't it the most?
Bye - bye   Bye - byes.
Con - grad - u - la - tions.
Al - len Gins-berg, Ha - re Krish-na Ha - re, Ha - re Krish-na.

All   we___ are

say -   ing___   is give peace___ a

chance.___   All   we___ are

say -   ing___   is give peace___ a

HOW?

Words and Music
by JOHN LENNON

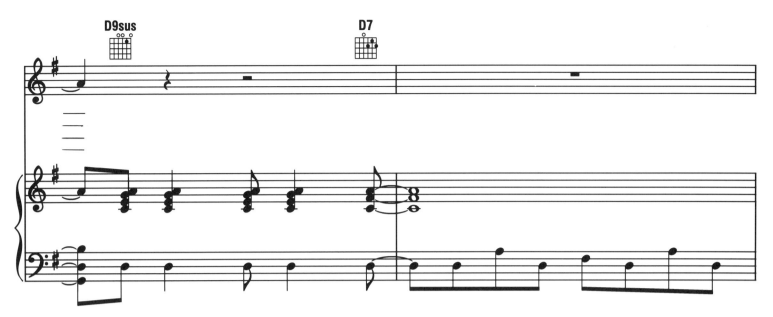

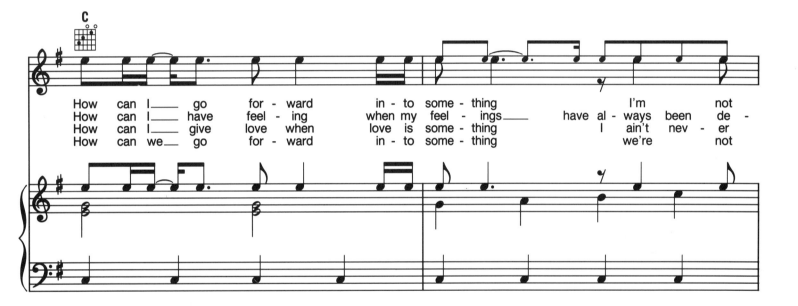

How can I___ go for - ward in - to some - thing I'm not
How can I___ have feel - ing when my feel - ings___ have al - ways been de -
How can I___ give love when love is some - thing I ain't nev - er
How can we___ go for - ward in - to some - thing we're not

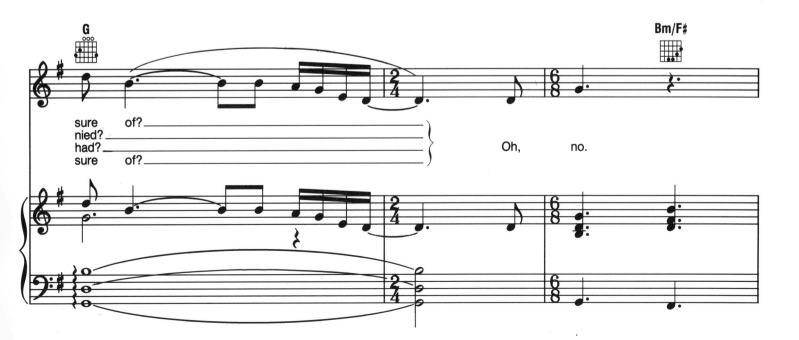

sure of?___
nied?___
had?___
sure of?___

Oh, no.

GOD

Moderately (♪ ♪ played as ⸌³ ♪ ♪)

Words and Music
by JOHN LENNON

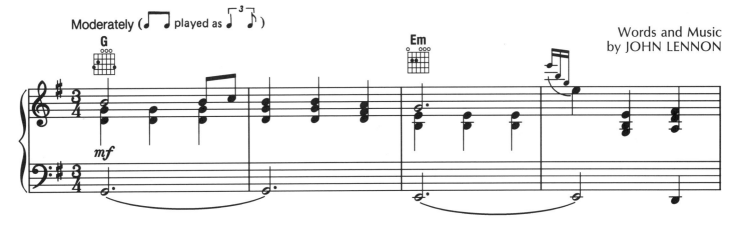

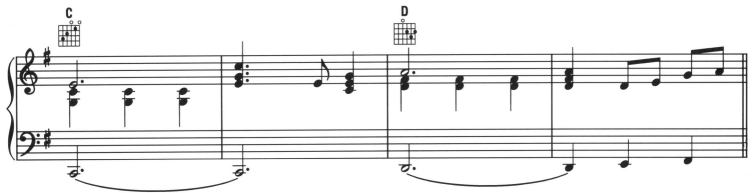

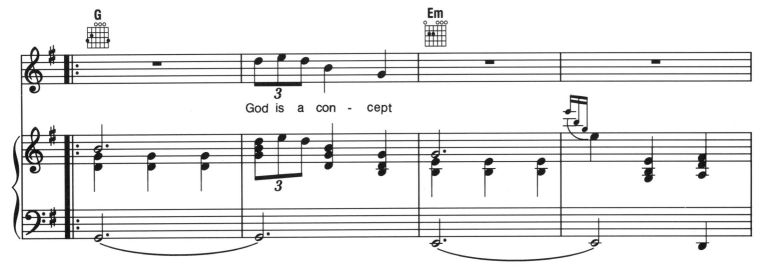

God is a con - cept

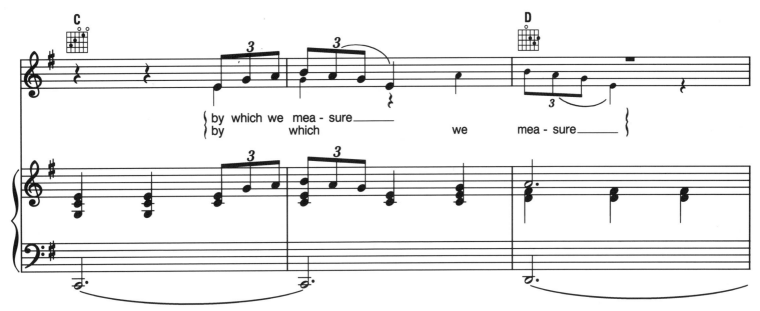

{ by which we mea - sure
{ by   which   we   mea - sure

57

Additional Lyrics

3. I don't believe in Bible.
4. I don't believe in Tarot.
5. I don't believe in Hitler.
6. I don't believe in Jesus.
7. I don't believe in Kennedy.
8. I don't believe in Buddha.
9. I don't believe in Mantra.
10. I don't believe in Gita.
11. I don't believe in Yoga.
12. I don't believe in Kings.
13. I don't believe in Elvis.
14. I don't believe in Zimmerman.
15. I don't believe in Beatles.

MOTHER

Words and Music by
JOHN LENNON

Slowly

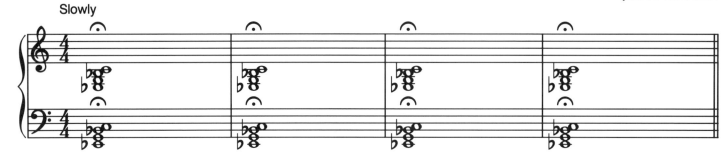

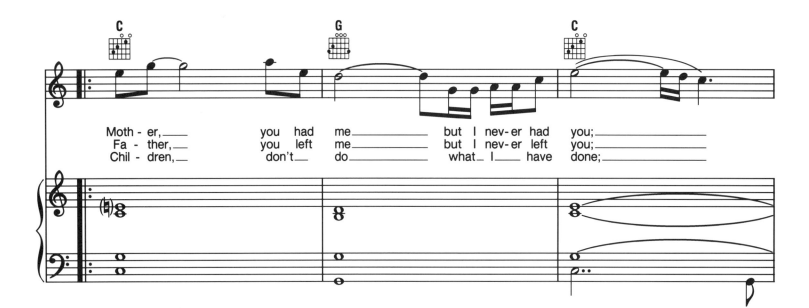

Moth - er,____ you had me____ but I nev-er had you;____
Fa - ther,____ you left me____ but I nev-er left you;____
Chil - dren,____ don't do____ what I____ have done;____

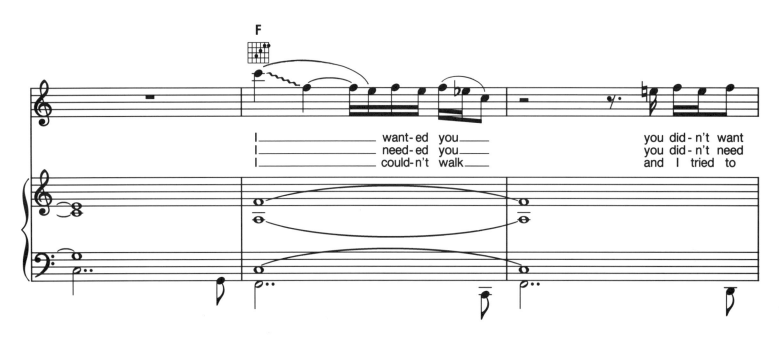

I ____ want-ed you ____ you did-n't want
I ____ need-ed you ____ you did-n't need
I ____ could-n't walk ____ and I tried to

STAND BY ME

Words and Music by BEN E. KING,
JERRY LEIBER and MIKE STOLLER

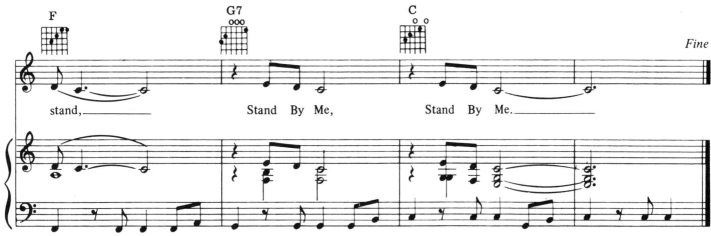

62

BEAUTIFUL BOY
(DARLING BOY)

Words and Music by
JOHN LENNON

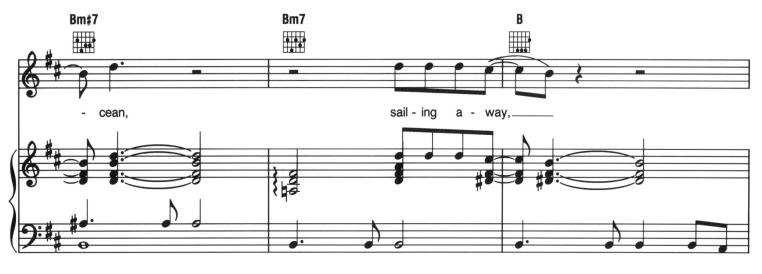

- cean, sailing a - way, _____

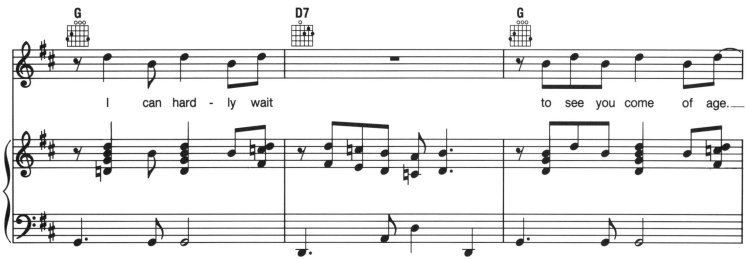

I can hard - ly wait to see you come of age.

_____ But I guess we'll both _____ just have _____ to be pa -

- tient. 'Cause it's a long _____ way to go,

JEALOUS GUY

Words and Music by
JOHN LENNON

Moderately Slow

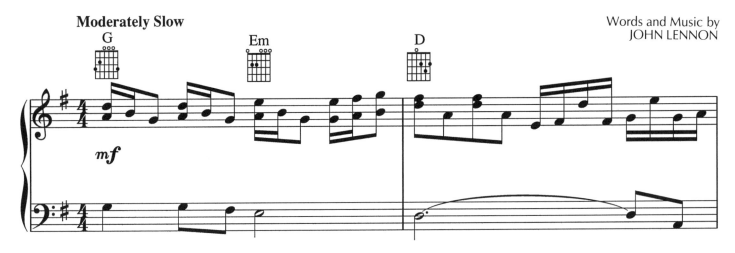

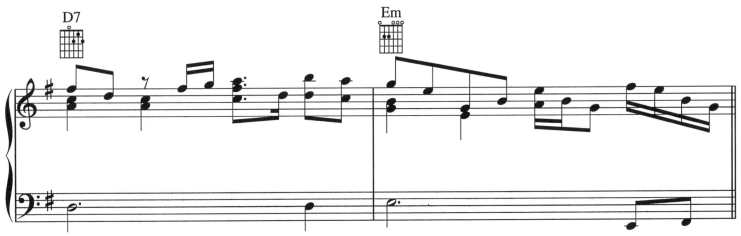

1. I was dream-ing of the past _____
2. I was feel-ing in - se - cure. _____
3. *Whistle*
4. I was trying to catch your eye. _____

WOMAN

Words and Music by
JOHN LENNON

Moderately slow

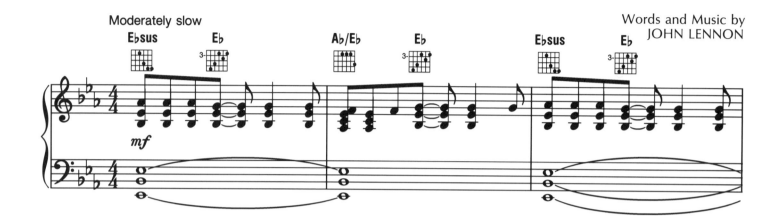

Wom-an, I can hard-ly ex-press
Wom-an, I know you un-der-stand

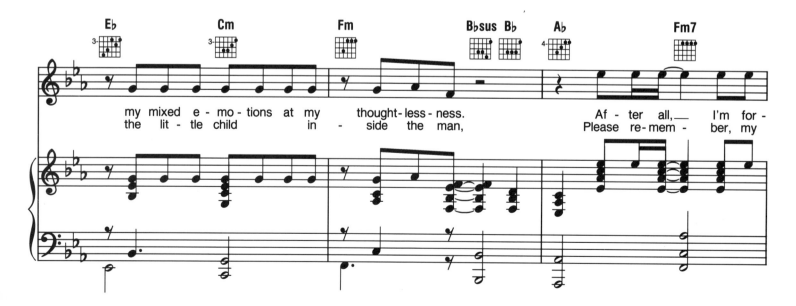

my mixed e-mo-tions at my thought-less-ness.
the lit-tle child in-side the man,

Af-ter all,___ I'm for-
Please re-mem-ber, my

(JUST LIKE)
STARTING OVER

Words and Music
by JOHN LENNON

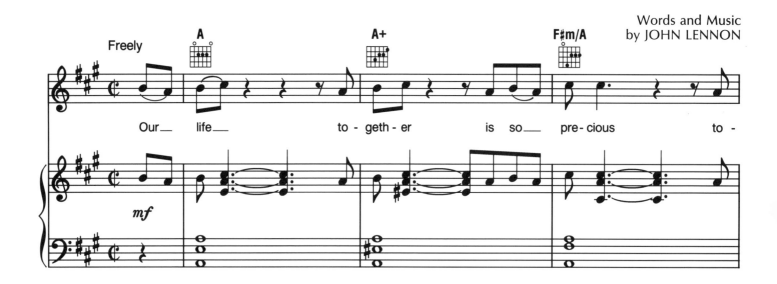

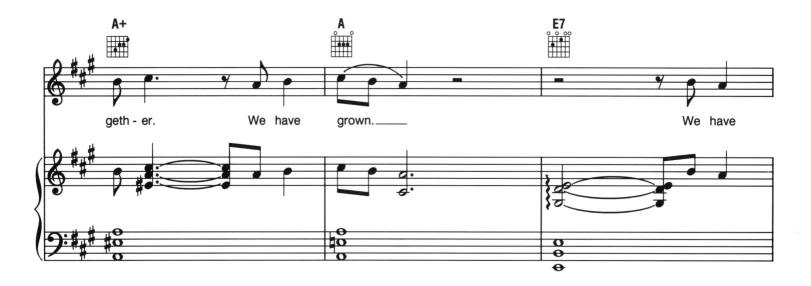

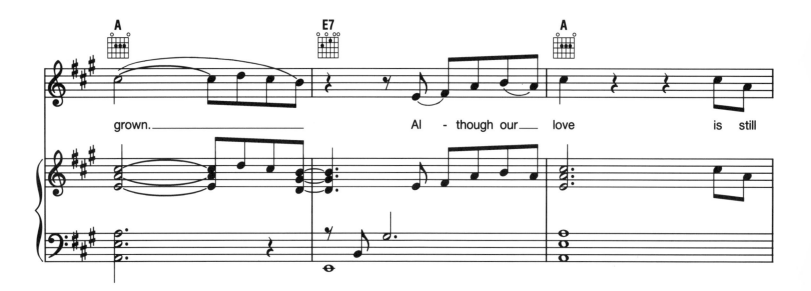

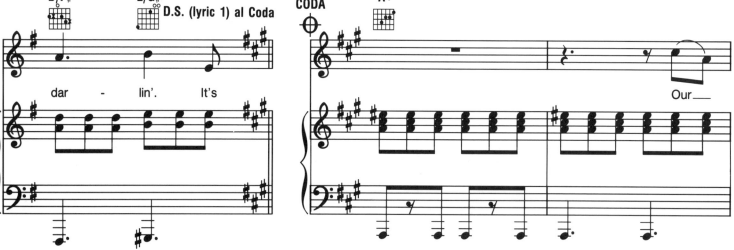

IMAGINE

Words and Music by
JOHN LENNON

tries.
ions.

It is-n't hard_____ to do._____
I won-der if you____ can._____

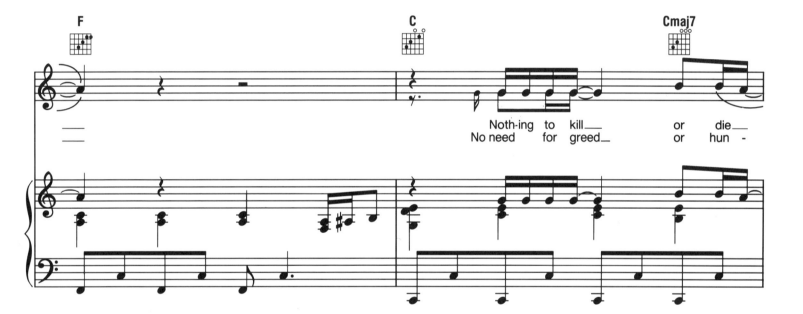

_____ for

Noth-ing to kill____ or die____
No need for greed____ or hun -

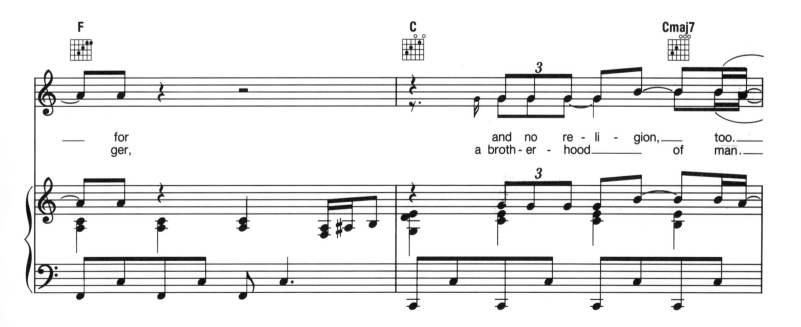

_____ for
ger,

and no re - li - gion,____ too.____
a broth-er - hood_____ of man.____